# Finding Your Path in Friendship

by

Sarafina James

Grosvenor House
Publishing Limited

All rights reserved
Copyright © Sarafina James, 2020

The right of Sarafina James to be identified as the author of this
work has been asserted in accordance with Section 78
of the Copyright, Designs and Patents Act 1988

The book cover is copyright to Sarafina James

This book is published by
Grosvenor House Publishing Ltd
Link House
140 The Broadway, Tolworth, Surrey, KT6 7HT.
www.grosvenorhousepublishing.co.uk

This book is sold subject to the conditions that it shall not, by way of
trade or otherwise, be lent, resold, hired out or otherwise circulated
without the author's or publisher's prior consent in any form of binding or
cover other than that in which it is published and
without a similar condition including this condition being imposed
on the subsequent purchaser.

This book is a work of fiction. Any resemblance to
people or events, past or present, is purely coincidental.

A CIP record for this book
is available from the British Library

ISBN 978-1-83975-263-6


Instagram: @author2020
Website: www.therealityoflife.online

# Dedicated to My Family

Husband – Jahnoy Oniesh James
Daughter – Janaelee Oneisha James
Son – Josias Jahnoy James
Mother – Evelyn Anderson

My family is my strength.
They're the reason I get up each morning to be a
better person,
and my love for them is certain.
Their love for me is embedded in my heart, and nothing
can ever tear us apart.
They're my peace, like the sound of an ocean.
And I am pleased to say, I've got a promotion.

The greatest gift I have ever received, without a moment
of feeling deceived.
God has truly blessed me with a special gift,
that no one could ever twist or shift.
So, I would like to thank them for assisting me in finding
my path in friendship.
What a wonderful feeling to know that I have found my way;
And I'm happy to show my dedication without delay.

# Contents

| | | |
|---|---|---|
| Chapter 1 | The Foundation | 1 |
| Chapter 2 | The Dream | 5 |
| Chapter 3 | Choosing the Right Friends | 8 |
| Chapter 4 | Moving to the Big Country | 15 |
| Chapter 5 | Friendships Can Change | 22 |
| Chapter 6 | Betrayal | 30 |
| Chapter 7 | Forgiveness | 38 |
| Chapter 8 | Types of Friends | 43 |
| Chapter 9 | My Husband Is My Best Friend | 57 |
| Chapter 10 | Self-Evaluation | 60 |
| Chapter 11 | How to Treat a Friend | 67 |
| Chapter 12 | Letting Go | 69 |
| Chapter 13 | The Realisation | 73 |
| Chapter 14 | Accepting and Adjusting | 76 |

# Chapter 1
# The Foundation

Is it true that we all need a friend? If so, what if you were to meet a person that proclaims that they don't have a friend or don't need a friend, would you think that was odd? Do you think a bad experience, perhaps some sort of betrayal, can cause a person to lose interest in friendship?

Betrayal is an act that most of us have experienced; you were either falsely accused of betraying a friend, or you suffered some form of betrayal. There are many reasons why people may feel betrayed because everyone has a unique perspective on life, which should be respected. As we delve more into the story of friendship, we will get into details about how it feels to be betrayed, why it hurts so much, and if it can be forgiven.

What if I was to say I knew someone who stopped trusting people from the age of 16? One bad experience caused her to lose interest in friendship. The person confessed she had 12 brothers and sisters and refused to play with them because there were too many of them; is this even a reason for not playing with your siblings? Could it be that she didn't like humans, or that she was self-centred? It is very hard to find a reasonable explanation for why the person was the way they were. There were times she was known for being selfish due to her isolation, but if people took the time to know her, they would discover that she is a person with a big heart who loves to help her family, friends, and even strangers.

This person stopped trusting mankind after she felt betrayal for the first time. In the 1970s, when school was over, it was a priority that you headed straight home because if you didn't, you would be in serious trouble with your parents.

The person made her first friend in the community who she could travel home with. One day on her way home, she was waiting at the bus stop with her friend when someone she knew saw her and began to have a conversation with her. While they were talking, her friend who she had travelled with got onto the bus, stuck her head out of the window and waved goodbye with a smirk on her face.

The person explained that, at that moment, she knew that she could never trust her again. The friend could have warned her that the bus was there; instead, she waved goodbye. Her friend knew the trouble she would be in if she arrived home late. She said that the next day her ex-friend approached her, and she ignored her without giving a reasonable explanation as to why she had ended the friendship. This experience changed the person's mindset towards making friends for life. Especially when she got a whopping from her parents and had to wash dishes for a week. This entailed her climbing up and down a hill to go to the river to collect water and carrying it on top of her head. This was her main duty in the morning, at noon and at night. Her brothers and sisters felt like kings and queens, and they occasionally teased her when they had the opportunity.

She confessed that on some days, she felt like breaking all the dishes, but she cherished her life more. This was the worst punishment she could have, because on a normal week when it was her time to wash dishes, she refused to eat dinner to skip her turn. I could just imagine how her fingers wrinkled after washing every single, plate, cup, piece of cutlery, and pot.

As she grew older, she learnt how to keep people at a distance. 'Hi, how are you, and bye,' was her motto, she admitted to some great people she'd met who were always willing to give a helping hand. She stressed that when you meet good people in your life, who require nothing from you and are kind-hearted and humble, never forget to show gratitude. She showed her gratitude by calling and checking up on them occasionally, but she never got too close. She said, "Friendship works better when it's at a distance; neither party has expectations, just a helping hand when needed."

I believe that she struggled to connect with people because she didn't know how to connect with her siblings. Some people aren't sociable, but when you had a conversation with her, she came across as friendly. I often wondered if she would have had a different perspective on friendship if she had taken the time to express to her ex-friend how she felt, and an apology was made.

Friendship is like being in a relationship, communication is the key! Ineffective communication can create misunderstandings, missed opportunities, conflict, mistrust, or even cause you to lose a friend. Now if you valued a friend as much as I do, losing a friend can affect you emotionally, mentally, and physically.

After she told me the story, I thought to myself, how could one bad experience ruin the prospect of making or keeping a friend. After all, having a friend meant the world to me because I was an only child. Having a friend made me feel valuable. I was always alone at home, although I grew up with my first cousin, who lived across the road from me. She always pushed me away due to the age gap, but I still loved going over to her house, hoping that one day she would give me some attention. Unfortunately, she never showed any interest. She was the only family I could play with, because my extended family lived in Jamaica, while I was born on a small island called St. Maarten. I didn't have a close family member that I could cling on to as a friend, so I had to go friend-hunting to fill that gap.

I could have turned to my mother, but it wouldn't be the same. We all know until you become an adult, you are more likely to value your mother's friendship. Let's be honest, having a friend can make you feel appreciated, valued and fulfilled. It's a beautiful feeling to know you have someone you can call on when you are down, stressed, disappointed, or even to vent.

Every person that I classed as a friend, I saw as a sister, a sister I never had. I convinced myself that they were my sister, and when it didn't work out, it affected me in an abnormal way. It affected my sleeping habits, and it would also cause me to have random conversations with myself about the situation. I could not rest until I had resolved the situation, and I would try to find wrong in what I did and make an apology for the friendship's sake. This was a behaviour I pursued until I was about 25 years old.

Psychological research claims that our childhood experience has a profound influence on who we are as adults. So, I challenge you to search deep into your childhood memories and see how your childhood experiences have caused you to be the friend you are today and what kind of friends you are attracted to. For example, the person I described previously eliminated friendship from her life and focused on associates. She was no longer interested in friendship after experiencing betrayal.

# Chapter 2
# The Dream

The greatest dream of my life was to have siblings. I've always admired siblings playing, teasing, and arguing with each other. I was reminded by others how lucky I was to be an only child and how they wished they were in my shoes. Remarks like this always amazed me, because in my eyes, anyone who had a sibling was very blessed. Having a companion is one of the greatest gifts you can have, it always conquers the feeling of loneliness.

I have never met a sibling who didn't wish they were an only child. They complained about their siblings intruding in their space, using their stuff, how annoying they were, and the list can go on and on. I guess this is something I will never understand, and it frustrates me because I have never really experienced what it is to have a sibling. I thought to myself, why they would want this lonely life that I have? When you are at home, the house is so quiet you can hear a pin drop. No matter what they said, I knew deep down inside their hearts, they loved their siblings unconditionally.

Jeff Brown stated, and I quote, "Words are powerful, they can crush a heart, or heal it. They can shame a soul or liberate it. They can shatter dreams or energise them. They can obstruct connection or invite it. They can create defences or melt them. We must use our words wisely."

I dreamt of someone being in my space. I wanted to scream at someone, "Get out of my room!" I wanted to share my toys, food or even love with someone. I believed this was how my kindness started to develop by fantasising about the life of an imaginary sibling. I was always willing to help and share with my friends who I thought were my sisters; the sisters who were a made-up fantasy in my mind. I convinced myself that siblings should always be kind and loving to each other, but this is not always the case. This was a dream that I was willing to make my reality!

I do not believe that every child who has no siblings is as delusional as I was. I knew quite of few who enjoyed being an only child because they got everything, and they didn't have to share love, attention, or toys. Life was great for them! An only child is known to be spoiled, I cannot relate because my mom never spoiled me, she made sure I was well taken care of and didn't lack anything. She even went the extra mile to give me a little bit of privilege, for example taking me on holidays.

Your sibling will always be your blood, and if there is a disagreement, nothing can change the fact that you are blood-related. But when you have a friend, and you have a disagreement, it is never guaranteed that you will remain friends. The choice is yours; you decide whether you want to pursue the friendship or not. You can choose your friends, but you cannot choose your family.

I wouldn't say I was jealous of or malicious to others, it was more of an admiration, like 'aww look at them'. When I left the outside world and closed my door, it was just me with the television and my schoolbooks. I had nobody to make jokes with, nobody to argue with, or tease, or even play with. Things became very lonely as I got older.

My daughter was able to live the dream I always wanted. When I had my firstborn, and she was two years old, I realised that she was all alone. She had no one to play with, and when we visited someone and they had a child, she always cried to stay. One day I put her in the garden to play while I was washing the dishes, I looked up and saw her looking around in the garden like she was lost. I felt sad to see her in the garden all by herself and flashbacks of my lonely childhood came rushing back. I immediately had the conversation with my husband and told him I thought it was time we had another child. He happily agreed and then came our son. Although my daughter was looking forward to having a sister, she was happy to have a baby brother. Watching them together fills my heart with joy because I know she will always have somebody. They play, fight, argue, and all the usual stuff siblings do. I can feel my daughter's pain when her brother is always in her space, but in my mind, it's always better than being alone. My kids' bond is always a confirmation that I can be healed, but the question is how long it will take for me to accept my healing.

My aim is to grow them to stick together and be loving to each other no matter what. It might not turn out that they follow the principles I implemented in them, but I can only hope that they do.

Take this moment to reflect on how blessed you are to have a sibling. I know some may not see it as a blessing, but I know that you have shared some good moments with your sibling(s). It took me a while to reflect on how blessed I am to have a mother to look after me. We are all blessed in different ways, and we should always appreciate our blessings. As a teenager, I didn't appreciate having a mother to look after me because I was too busy creating a sisterly bond. I love my mom dearly, but I never really had the time to reflect and understand what was going on. I guess, as a child, you wouldn't have developed enough life experience to understand life properly.

# Chapter 3
# Choosing the Right Friends

When we were growing up, our parents emphasised how important it was to choose our friends wisely. I am sure there were some friends our parents absolutely loved and adored, while there were others that they thought were bad company, ill-mannered and lacking in respect or self-integrity. Growing up in the Caribbean, most parents mainly judged a friend by their spirit, this was done by analysing a person's energy. They had a saying 'my spirit doesn't take him'. The term 'him' can refer to either a boy or a girl.

With regard to choosing my friends, I would rather rewind to when I was in high school; not that my primary friends were irrelevant, they were very relevant, in fact, they were great! A child's favourite memory about primary school was playtime. My primary friends were important in developing my social skills and my self-esteem, and they also gave me some sense of belonging.

I prefer to start at high school and upwards because, at that stage, I had more understanding about the concept of life.

I met my best friend when I was 14 years old. We ended up being in the same class, and we got to know each other day by day. We recognised how much we had in common, and the relationship began to get stronger. My bestie was a very popular person, she knew everyone, and everyone wanted to associate themselves with her. I was not good at making new friends, the people I knew at high school were the people I associated with at primary school. I always tried to stick to the people I knew, but my primary friends ended up being in different classes, which forced me to meet new people. As I got older, the people that I classed as close friends became more like acquaintances. Losing and making new friends is not necessarily a bad thing, it's a part of life. Losing a friend can have quite a few benefits, whether they were a good or bad friend. Stay tuned to know how and why.

I classed my bestie as the perfect friend. Our relationship grew closer and closer, and at that point, I knew I had found a sister. Being around her caused me to be more sociable and have lots of connections. This was a friend that cared about me, listened to me, showed me respect, and she was always there for me no matter the circumstances. She has a good heart, and she is a good person, and that is enough for me. Yes, at times, we had disagreements, but we argued with respect. We shared our most intimate secrets, and there was total honesty.

Honesty is very important in any relationship, there is a saying that 'honesty is the best policy'. Some friends may be brutally honest and think that they are being authentic. The right way to be honest, especially if it may come across as offensive, is to think about what you are going to say and say what you need to say in a respectful manner, and make a minor apology for the way it makes the person feel. There should never be an intent to hurt another friend. I am sure there are cases where you might have said something, and it came across as a bit harsh, just try to acknowledge it and make an apology. To be honest with each other, both parties must be open to that honesty. In my opinion, if a friend shows signs of dishonesty, then there is no point in continuing the friendship. Honesty is the foundation of maintaining a good friendship.

I must admit that there are quite a few people who do not understand the meaning of honesty. Honesty is about being able to keep to your word by telling the truth and communicating freely. My best friend and I were both open to being honest with each other, which empowered us to develop a consistency in how we present facts.

She was a very supportive friend, we did everything together: we had sleepovers, we went shopping together, we paid for each other's lunch if one was short of cash. I can even remember when we were asked by a friend if we wanted to try marijuana, we pulled each other aside and discussed if we should or not. We made the decision to give it a try, just to see what everyone was so crazy about, then we made a promise that we would only do it this one time. This was a true and real friend; the bond was inseparable. I am sure the majority of us have experienced what true friendship feels like.

There are a few who believe that 'if the friendship didn't last, the person wasn't a true friend in the first place'. I have mixed feelings about this, I tend to disagree. Can you end up not being friends with someone that you once classed as a true friend? Can one disappointment or betrayal cause you not to see the authenticity of that person? Could it be that we are so focused on the bad that it overtakes the good in the person? What does a true friend mean? Everyone has a different definition, but to me, a true friend means someone who will always be there to support you, give you a helping hand, always have your back, will never judge you, will tell you the truth even when it hurts, but your feelings are taken into consideration. A true friend is someone trustworthy and reliable.

There was a time when I felt I disappointed my best friend. I never asked her if she felt betrayed when the incident happened, I guess if she did, she would have told me. I can recall her explaining to me about a girl who lived near our school, who she had a disagreement with. One day, the girl came to our school with a gang of friends, and they made a circle, and as I was walking to the bus stop, I saw this commotion. When I ran to look, my best friend and this girl were fighting. I instantly got ready to jump in, I dropped everything, but I was stopped by the girl's friend. She grabbed the collar of my shirt very firmly, and when I looked up at the girl, I was shocked. She was very tall, taller than an average teenager, she must have been at least five feet eight inches, and she also had weight. She gripped my shirt tightly and said, "It's a one-to-one fight, let it be fair." My friend lost the fight and I was devastated. I asked myself, W*hy didn't I fight the girl to help my friend?* The truth was, I feared how big she was and that she would finish me if I tried. I knew I couldn't win if I fought her. I saw myself as a coward for not helping my best friend to win the fight. The next day, people would ask me why I didn't help my friend, and how could I allow that to happen to her? I knew I had no valid reason, and a sense of disappointment would come over me. Years later, I confessed to my bestie how I felt I let her down, and she assured me I had no reason to feel that way. Her initial words were, "You win some and you lose some."

Thinking back on the incident, I knew that some people would have ended the friendship. However, I would have understood if she did due to my cowardice.

There was a time when I felt disappointed by my best friend, which is when I repeated the third form. She passed to the fourth form and made new friends. Sometimes when our best friend makes new friends, it can either break or make the relationship. When she met these friends, she had to split her time with them and me. I felt as if she didn't have much time for me anymore. I guess you can call it jealousy; I was jealous that we didn't spend as much time together as we used to. The situation was understandable because we were not in the same class, but I didn't like the feeling that I might lose my best friend. I started to cling on to this new girl in my class, and she became the companion friend. She also was not in the same class with the friends she once had, so I guess we were both using each other for company.

We sat together, we walked together, and we joked around a lot. It took us a while to be open with each other, but as you know, friendship is built over time until trust is gained by both parties. I grew to love her as a sister, but I always sensed that she was not very happy overall. I had a strong feeling that she was going through a lot at home, but she wouldn't open up to me. She only let me know what she wanted me to know, she would tell half a story and put a twist on it. This friend trusted nobody; it took her at least eight years to truly open up to me and to trust me with her fears, secrets, and problems. She loved to laugh; I think this was her coping mechanism to ignore the seriousness of life. If she found something funny, she could laugh for five minutes straight, and I would like to emphasise on how loud her laughter was.

She got pregnant at the age of 16, and she had to drop out of school due to the circumstances. I made it my duty to ensure I maintained the relationship with her. I knew she had no true friends at school, I wanted to be her friend, and I wanted her to take me for a loyal friend that she could trust. I believed she took me for a friend, but only to an extent. The companion friend was the strongest teenager I knew. Even through her bad times, she kept fighting, her circumstances did not hold her back. One thing that I admired about her was that she gave her daughter the best life she could, even at such a young age. I really admire her strength.

As I started to get more freedom from my mom, one day I decided to go to the community centre in the district, to watch a basketball game. This is where I made a new friend in my district. She was understanding and funny and had a great personality. She was older than I was, and she was very knowledgeable and quite experienced. She was the experienced friend; I admired her knowledge, and overtime we built a strong friendship.

I was over the moon that I had a friend near where I lived, so every chance I got I would walk down to her house and sit on her porch, and we would talk, laugh, and discuss our life experiences. I chose her to be my friend because she was a good-hearted person with knowledge.

When I was about 17 years old, I joined a crew that called themselves 'the buddy crew'. They were known to be rebels, even though my true personality was not who they were. I am sure in the eyes of the public, they saw me as a rebel also, but I ensured that I was true to myself by not giving in to peer pressure. It is a good experience to have a circle of friends, and you might think they are your true friends, but sometimes they are not. My best friend was also a part of this clique; somehow, we managed to maintain our friendship by having a balance when it came to outside friendships or relationships. I knew this was a group of friends I just wanted to have fun with.

Overall, I would like to believe that I picked my friends wisely. What more could I have wanted as a teenager, I had the bestie, the companion friend, the knowledgeable friend and a crew to have fun with occasionally? Don't get me wrong, I knew other people as well, but these were the main people in my life that I associated with on a daily basis.

Now there was a point where I had to say goodbye to all these beautiful people in my life because I had to go aboard to study. The question is, after going away, who remained in my life?

We think we have chosen the right friends to share our life with, but a lifetime of friendship is never guaranteed. There is this saying, 'some people are only in your life for a season'. I honestly hate that saying, because I do not let people in my life if I know they are only going to be there for a short period of time, but I acknowledge that there is some truth in it.

I think people feel making the right choice in friendship means that the friendship must last forever. I tend to disagree with this because we can make a good choice in a friend and it just wasn't meant to be.

How do we know if we have made the right choice? Truth be told, we don't. Sometimes it takes a disagreement or a betrayal to break a friendship and, just like any relationship, both partners must be willing to sustain the connection. In other words, both parties must put in the effort for it to work.

I have met people who chose to not have close friends because it's too much stress, too much expectation, and too much work to sustain the relationship. I must admit it can be stressful if you find a friend who causes you a lot of grief.

I currently have a friend who explained that after various issues with friends, she pulls out a checklist when she meets people. This checklist happens to be in her mind. She explained if the person is not ambitious with a car or job, it's a big X for her, meaning that they cannot be her friend. I never really understood the checklist, but when you reach a certain stage in your life, some stresses that come with friendship can be very draining, so with that being said, I do understand why she pulls out her checklist.

Can this checklist save her from being hurt by a friend? The answer is no. People can be very deceiving, and it can take years before you know someone's true side. The true sides tend to come out when things change or when something out of the ordinary occurs.

It's very easy to deceive me because I am a naive person, all I need is a sign of a good heart and interest that you want to be my friend, and I will welcome you with open arms. Over the years, I have learnt that this is not a good trait to have when meeting people.

I think it is important to look at traits or signs when choosing a friend.

Choose friends:

- Who have the same values
- Who have the same mindset
- Who are go-getters
- Who celebrate your success
- Who motivate you to do better
- Who are willing to give and take and not just take

Unfortunately, choosing good traits in a friend still doesn't guarantee a lifetime of friendship!

# Chapter 4
# Moving to the Big Country

Moving to another country can be very scary and unpredictable. When I came to the UK, I was very excited to study to be an accountant. Primarily, I had to be open-minded to making adjustments and adapting to the lifestyle, the people, the culture, and the weather. There is a big disparity when you compare an island that is only 37 square miles to the UK. For example, in the Caribbean, we knew all our neighbours from the top of the road to the end of the road, and it was a must that you greeted each one of them when you saw them. The UK is a bit different; your neighbours are the ones on the left or right, and you're lucky to even get a hello.

I can remember going on the bus in the UK and saying a very big 'morning' to everyone, and no one answered. I immediately thought to myself that the people on this bus have no manners. I was told by a family member that global greetings on the bus are not needed. How embarrassing, right! This was something new because back home, if you didn't greet everyone on the bus, people would give you bad looks or even talk under their breath and say, "You lack manners."

Whatever adaptations and adjustment I had to make, I ensured it was done because I was determined to accomplish my goals. Initially, I thought England was great, it was a whole new adventure, and I was looking forward to starting over. Sometimes people would ask me why I would leave my island of sunshine to come to this country that is known for unpredictable weather. I really didn't understand what they were talking about until years of living in this country. I must admit, I took my sunshine for granted.

I was introduced to a family friend who went to the same college as I did. She was very friendly, and she showed me around, greeted me when she saw me at college, and she even asked me to join her from time to time. She was fascinated by the way I talked because I had a strong St. Maarten accent. Knowing that one person made me feel like I wasn't a foreigner at college.

I was drawn to her at college because she was the only person I knew, and as I said before, I was not a person that knew how to make new friends. I was not very sociable, if someone showed me interest, I would then show them interest. I wouldn't go out of my way to do so. Eventually, her friends became my friends, in fact, one of her associates became my close friend. This associate was a popular person, and everyone admired her; she was a very beautiful girl.

When I came to the UK, I was 18 years old, and I loved going out to parties to have fun with my friends. My friends and I shared the same interests, and I would say fun was our middle name.

In the beginning, I was closer to the first person I was introduced to, I called her the helpful friend. We did everything together and we had quite a few sleepovers, but an incident happened that allowed me to draw closer to the popular friend. I was partially accused of stealing money from her parent's house. Being considered as a suspect for a theft is not a nice feeling although I understood why, but I still had a very weird feeling inside my stomach, especially when I knew I was innocent. This changed our relationship because we spent less time together, so I started to cling to the popular friend I was introduced to. Over time, the popular friend became my new British/Jamaican bestie.

She was an only child on her mother's side, and I thought this was an opportunity where I could potentially have a sister again. I started to open up to this friend, and once I trusted her,

I told her everything about myself; we both started to learn about each other while spending a huge amount of time together. I saw the good in her and I really enjoyed being around her; after all, she introduced me to my first boyfriend in England, who eventually became my husband after three years.

Just before I came to England, I was introduced to my baby brother on my father's side. I can remember when my father told me that he was born, I was so excited, and I thought, at last, I finally have what I always wanted, a sibling. My father and I did not have a healthy relationship, and I could count on my fingers how many times I saw my baby brother. One day it hit me that our relationship could never be the same as other siblings who grew up and lived together. I applaud parents that ensure that outside siblings are united and can create a strong bond.

If I remember rightly, when I came to the UK, he was only a couple of months old. There was no way I could have a relationship with my brother because my father and I did not have a stable relationship, and in addition, I lived thousands of miles away.

I sometimes questioned why I hadn't tried to maintain a relationship with my sibling, since I wanted one so badly. I concluded that it was too late to fill the gap of a missing sibling because of the massive age gap and because I now reside in the UK. Do you think I am making an excuse because of fear? Or could it be that I just didn't want to acknowledge him, and I had got used to being an only child? I often ask myself these questions, but I mostly think it's fear.

Why am I scared? Truth be told, I am not sure. I often wonder if it's because I know that we won't have that strong bond. Or is it that I am scared to face my dad about what happened in the past? The sad thing about the situation is that this little prince is innocent and is in-between the unstable relationship my dad and I share. I am finding it very hard to figure out a way to fix it due to circumstances. I acknowledge that this is a chapter in my life where I need to find closure.

Eventually, my first cousin who I grew up with maintained some sort of communication when I lived in the UK; she was finally interested. She had a lot of trust issues with people, but somehow, she drew closer to me and we began to keep in regular contact. We ensured our kids grew together on social media, so they could have a relationship too. Over the years our relationship grew into something great, and we learnt to appreciate each other as sisters, rather than cousins.

The companion friend and I maintained contact and, little by little, she started to open up to me and vice-versa. When we were friends in high school, I used to wonder why she was so secretive with her life, but at the age of 27, I learnt that she was just protecting her heart, a quality I wished I had. I believe that I am too open about my life experiences, and I always try and use my experiences to help others in their lives.

As I grew older, I admired how my companion friend kept her problems, whether good or bad, to herself. As I got to know her, I realised that she was also a thinker and a worrier. Could it be because she is not a person to open up to receive advice or help? Can these behaviours often lead to depression? I am no expert in psychology, but I like to try and understand why people are the way they are, so I can adjust and connect.

I think keeping things bottled up can lead to depression and can be very unhealthy for the internal body. When you express these feelings, you are acknowledging how you feel openly, and someone who is listening can understand and help to find a solution to those problems. When you do not express your feelings, it can make you feel all alone, and often many people are going through the same thing as you are. That doesn't mean that you should be happy that you have someone similar going through the same situation, but the person's journey and how they got over the situation can become a great help to you. I have met someone who takes pleasure from other people's problems or sadness; if they were going through obstacles in their lives, they would get excited to know that you are also going through difficulties that brings you pain.

Have you ever heard that misery loves company? If you have a friend that only cares to know about your problems instead of your successes, ask yourself why?

My companion friend grew to trust me with her problems, whether good or bad, and I know at times she feels relief. I might not be able to fix everything, but just the thought that I am a phone call away helps. She can call any hour of the day, and she has always made herself available to my needs as well. Friendship is a two-way road!

If you cannot find a friend or family member you can trust, try and seek some professional help, or research and see if there is a free service that you can utilise. There are so many different techniques you can use to express your feelings, such as writing a letter on paper and expressing how you feel and watching it burn. I have tried this strategy and it feels awesome. It almost felt like I had burnt the problem away. Watching the paper burn forced me to confront my problems because the burnt paper was a representation that the problem no longer exists. It's always worth trying something because bottling up feelings can cause stress, anger, sadness or even lead to suicidal thoughts or actions. To share your feelings with someone helps to organise your thoughts, and it is the first step in changing your life.

I must confess I have unfolded some of my feelings to people I thought cared about me. I will warn you that there are good pretenders out there who act as if they care, but in the end, they just want to know what is going on in your life. Having the ability to discern these people can help to prevent opening up to the wrong people. Yes, it is important that I found the right person to go to, but when I thought about it, it was best I opened up rather than keeping it inside and then allowed karma to take its course.

My best friend and I did not maintain contact, which might come as a shock, it even puzzles me as well when I think about it. Would you pose the question that if she was such a best friend why didn't we keep the relationship going? You might think that we weren't truly best friends in the first place. I admit, the situation between me and my best friend is very complicated.

Have you ever had a friend that you do not communicate with regularly, maybe six months or a year might pass before you check in? Well, this was us, but the beauty of this friendship is when we finally got in contact, we updated each other about life. The foundation has been built between us and feels so unbreakable because we share the same morals and almost have the same personality. We tend to say it's because we have the same star sign (Aquarius). If we were to meet up again, it would be just like the old days. Based on my experience in the UK, I often wonder if we would have remained best friends if I was still living in St. Maarten.

I remain in contact with one person from the buddy crew. Every so often we check on each other to see how life is treating us and offer support, if needed.

The knowledgeable friend and I also remained in contact with each other, and we also talked about life and motivated each other. We don't talk every day, but we were always there to support each other through difficult situations. She remained the person I went to for advice.

When I got pregnant, I connected with one of my old classmates who currently lives in Holland. She was pregnant about the same time as me. From there, we shared our experience of being moms and how it felt. It is always nice to have a friend that you can connect and relate to. Our relationship grew based on positivity and real-life situations. We planned trips to visit each other which allowed our kids to spend time together. She is an amazing person who is all about self-growth, evaluation, and positive energy. I believe our friendship works well because we both share the same morals.

Coming to a big country all by myself caused me to draw closer to my mom, and it also allowed me to do a lot of self-evaluation. I believed leaving my mom affected me mentally, I left the only person that I truly knew that cared about me.

Our relationship improved day by day, my mom eventually became my true best friend. A friend that will never leave nor forsake me.

Growing up, we might not see our parents as our friends, but as we get older and start to experience life for ourselves, they become the person we turn to for advice or a helping hand. Some of us may not have a parent to talk to, but I do believe various people are placed in our lives to assists us to get through. The cycle of life allows us to meet different people on a daily basis.

# Chapter 5
# Friendships Can Change

Friendships tend to change when two people grow apart because their lives have taken a sudden or unusual turn. People are always scared when they hear the word change, it is not necessarily a bad thing. Being open to change shows that you are open to face and overcome any challenges. When your friendship evolves, look at it as an opportunity to embrace new experiences and become a better person. The complexity of friendship develops as an adult when you are in your early 20's, as at that stage, you begin to make life-changing decisions.

*Having a baby*

I found it very hard to find a guy who I was interested in, so the popular friend introduced me to my husband to be. One of the main things that changed our friendship was when I got pregnant, and after I had my firstborn because I couldn't party as much as I did. My relationship with her was mainly based on going out, having fun, and entertaining ourselves.

The way I saw life was different, for some reason kids tend to have that kind of effect on you. I had my princess when I was 21 years old. Even though I had her young, it seems like once she came into my arms, I matured very quickly. I wanted to set an example to her, and I wanted her to look up to me and be the best person she could be. I didn't want her to see Mommy going out to parties every weekend. I wanted to dedicate my entire time to her, and I didn't want to miss a moment.

My whole life changed, and I didn't have much family in the area to allow me to take a break. It is highly recommended that mothers should try to get a break to recharge their batteries. I believe that recharging your batteries helps you to be the mom that you want to be for your kids. For me, going out and having fun had to take a back seat!

I had two main friends in the UK: the popular friend and the helpful friend. The helpful friend lived three hours away, so we hardly ever saw each other, but somehow we managed to keep a connection through my life-changing situations.

In times like this, some friends might find it hard to adapt to the new you, because they didn't understand the depths of what you are going through as a new mom and they have no set responsibilities. They might come across as if they have failed you as a friend, but sometimes until they experience it for themselves, they will have no knowledge of how to be there for you.

I also believe that living in the UK forces people to be a bit selfish because of how the system is set up. Everyone is working, and due to the weather, people may become demotivated to do anything or visit anyone.

In most cases, the friend who failed to understand your new life might feel like they lost you as a friend. Friendship is like a relationship, spending time together can be an important factor in keeping the relationship strong, but time might not always be on your side when it comes to maintaining the friendship. Friends need to understand that just because your situation has changed, that doesn't mean the friendship is not real.

If you are that person feeling left out because your friend doesn't have time for you due to having kid(s): visit the friend, help her out, whether it's by cleaning, washing the dishes, holding the baby while she rests or even offering a wine night at her house. Do not just drift away and feel isolated; please note, in times like this, your friend needs your support and any support will be appreciated. I think many of us can confess that having a child caused us to lose a lot of friends. I didn't lose a friend when I had a child, but we drifted a bit from each other. I think it's important to have friends who also have children because it gives you the opportunity to learn from each other's maternal experiences. Motherhood can be classed as the most challenging situation to adapt and adjust to, and for some it may be impossible to relate to, if they are yet to experience it.

## Religion

Giving my life to God and accepting the Lord as my personal saviour also affected our friendship. My views and engagements changed, and we no longer shared the same insight on life. The partying life was one hundred percent over! We enjoyed eating out from time to time, and we occasionally went shopping. She is a fun and vibrant person, so when I decided to give my life to God, in addition to having a child, it allowed our friendship to change. Somehow, we held on to maintaining and sustaining our connection. Religion should never dictate a friendship because we should never try to impose our beliefs on others.

## Cultures

We always argued, and often we could not see eye to eye because we had a different outlook on life. I often wondered if it was because we were too involved in each other's personal life. I do not think either of us had a friend that we argued so much with. Could it be because we were from separate cultures? She is a Jamaican, and I am a St. Maartener, and most times we misinterpreted each other. Although we are from the Caribbean, we have different backgrounds. When people met us, they often say we argued like we were husband and wife. I saw her as my little sister even though we fought like animals; despite the circumstances, we shared a lot of good moments.

## Relationships

Being in a relationship with a partner can also affect your friendship, especially if the other party is single. A form of jealousy can develop because you are probably spending more time with your partner. Very often, friends tend to be jealous because you're in a relationship and they are not. It's important to reflect on and recognise both angles. Jealousy means feeling or showing an envious resentment of someone for their achievement, possessions, or perceived advantage. If someone can carry such feelings, this is not your friend. No matter the situation, a friend should always be happy for you.

I am sure a lot of us have experienced a jealous friend. I admit it is not easy to draw yourself away from the person or even confront them, but eventually, due to the jealous behaviour, it can destroy the friendship. It even changes the way you see the person altogether, and it might put a strain on the relationship. The open question is, what do you do when you have a jealous friend? One observation I've made in life is that I have never met a person who will admit to being jealous.

Most friends tend to be jealous because of the situations they are going through, or they might feel down about themselves. Before writing them off due to jealous remarks or behaviour, try to figure out what is causing them to behave in this manner. If you decide to talk to them about their behaviour, never accuse them of being jealous. Please note, no one admits to being jealous of anyone. Focus on the remarks they made or their actions towards the situation, explain to them how it made you feel. If you have accumulated years of friendship, instead of drifting away and acting strange, I believe it is more reasonable to give the person an explanation.

After becoming aware of their jealous behaviour, and a decision is made to continue the friendship, there may be a possibility that they will continue to have these traits. Trying to fix a relationship that has some jealousy is not worth it. But if you still refuse to terminate the friendship, the best option is to spend less time with them and expose less personal information.

There are friends who alienate themselves when they are in a new relationship. It may seem as if they have forgotten about your existence and will give their new partner their undivided attention. Falling in love caused them to forget who you are. I know this can be frustrating to watch but take heed that they haven't forgotten you, but they haven't mastered the skill of how to balance you in their life. We are all different, and when it comes to having friends, you must try to understand them, so you can have a healthier and more peaceful relationship.

When you are a teenager or in your early twenties, and you are in a relationship with someone, if you fail to enjoy the pleasures of life with your friends, you might feel overburdened and overwhelmed trying to sustain a relationship with your partner.

I advise any young person to live their life to its full capacity and create a balance with friendships and relationships. As you get older, you will live to regret that you didn't get to fully enjoy your youth. Sometimes, you end up not being with the person you fell in love with in your early days. Receiving love is the greatest gift, but it is not healthy to concentrate solely on your partner. Always have a friendship and a life alongside a relationship.

## *Starting a business*

Never mix business with friendship. I acknowledge there might be friends in this world who are able to work with each other and sustain a successful business. The majority of the time, if you decide to start a business with a friend, one will always have more drive than the other, meaning one will always do more than the other. Both parties need to be on the same page. If this is not the case, it can have a massive effect on the relationship, such as tensions, arguments, resentment or even a termination of the friendship.

Therefore, it is said, 'do not mix business with pleasure'. I admire friends who are working as a team to build a successful business together and manage to agree to disagree if needed. When working with friends, it is essential that both parties remain on the same page. They must be respectful, trustworthy, hardworking, humble, reliable, good with money, and have good communication and understanding skills. If you are thinking about going into business with a friend and they don't have these qualities, it is best to save your friendship by just remaining friends. If you decide to go into business knowing they lack some of these vital qualities, you are looking for destruction.

## *Work Commitments*

What if both friends are working and not having time for each other due to different work patterns? Is this something you can understand without feeling irritated? Life takes over and time is no longer your ally when it comes to sustaining a friendship. I think when you are in your early twenties, you tend not to understand that aspect of life, but as you get older, you tend to understand it's okay not to have time for your friends. Simple, petty stuff like this should never change years of friendship, but we know, in reality, it does. You might meet someone new who is available when you are free and you start to cling more to that person, so your actual friend becomes more like an associate.

## *Money*

Lending money to a friend who promised to pay you back can also change the friendship. There are several cases where friends are no longer friends due to a disagreement about money. My number one rule is, never lend a friend more than you can afford to lose.

## *Progression*

What about a friend who is elevating in his or her career and becoming more career-orientated and perhaps may come across as 'stuck up' or feel as if they are better than others? Is this a friend you cannot stand to be around, or is it you that cannot stand to see your friend's success because of jealousy?

I am not saying that there are not people who change because they are making more money and have a good job. If you are experiencing a friend like this, be happy to let them go because you no longer have the same values or morals and they are not being true to themselves.

I class these people as hypocrites. And if you are questioning yourself about pulling out of the friendship, ask yourself, "Do I want to maintain a fake friendship?" Sometimes people's view of life changes based on their success, but don't be alarmed.

## *Relocating*

Moving to a different country can affect a friendship, but with the technology that is available, it doesn't have to change. Both parties must be willing to maintain the relationship. As you can see, some of my friends and I remained in contact and some of us didn't. The connection of any long-distance friendship can be easily broken if taken for granted.

## *Morals and Values*

I believe as we get older, our mindset, goals, and morals change. Some of us might look for something greater to achieve in life. Often when your mind and heart is focused on higher levels, our friends might be content with where they are, and that is okay; but what is not okay is when your opinions and values lead to many disagreements. You may be evolving, while the person is stuck at the same place, where you left them.

Having the same morals and values is important when it comes to maintaining a healthy friendship because after a while it becomes toxic, especially if your friend cannot differentiate between right and wrong. Morals are a standard of behaviour; principals of right and wrong, and because we are all so different, we will therefore have different ethics.

If you change your lifestyle towards positive energy and it is having an effect on your friendship, then the other party hasn't fully evolved into maturity. This can be very frustrating to deal with, and it is best that you take a break to see what you both truly want. It might be that you guys will work out better as mutual friends rather than close friends. After all, why treat someone like an enemy when you shared so many memories with the person? It's time to make a choice, decide if it is worth pursuing.

# Chapter 6
# Betrayal

Truth be told, I have never truly experienced betrayal from a friend, but what I realised is that I have lost friendships due to a cycle of disagreements. Maybe I was betrayed but I never saw it as betrayal, or maybe I was good at choosing my friends. Who knows? Time will tell!

Every friend that I have lost was because of something I said or something they said. When I was 25 years old, I decided to let go of my first friend, I believe this is where I started to grow and started to see things differently. I have never been the person to let go of people even though I might be offended or hurt, it's always the other way around. I honestly believe I had an obsession with holding on to people.

I can remember letting go of a friend that talked to me in a vindictive way while giving a helping hand. At the age of 25, I had a big switch, it's very hard to pinpoint what exactly caused me to change. I think I was tired of being the old me and I wanted something new. The old person would have let these things slide, called, apologised and try to make amends, even though I knew I was not wrong. Anything to keep a long-lasting friendship, after all, I thought these people were my sisters. People always seem to let go of me with ease without it affecting them in any way. I guess it's because they did not have that crazy idea of me being their sibling. Like they say, there are always two sides to a story, but my reason was that I was tired of always making that initial move to fix a friendship.

When a friend treats you coldheartedly because you told them that you didn't like something they said to you, it really shows that friends are not guaranteed. If I knew that I would cause some form of offence, then I probably wouldn't have said anything. Then again, it is only fair that I express how I truly feel after 11 years of friendship. Thinking how the person responded to me did not affect me in any way, I began to get stronger and stronger in allowing things to be. I think I felt a sense of joy within me that this situation did not bring back the old habits of abnormality. I had so many minor incidents with people that nothing phased me anymore. Back in the day, something like that would get inside my mind and torment the life out of me, and I would have found a way to fix it. I learnt how to self-reflect on situations. I figured that maybe me expressing how I felt allowed her to feel like I saw her as a bad friend. Maybe she thought to herself, why bother with someone that could be hurt by something she said that was not intentional.

When I thought about it, I was okay with her decision. I probably caused her some sort of hurt. If there is one thing I deserve, it's a trophy, because I analysed the situation, and I didn't allow myself to be bothered with people who couldn't be bothered with me. If this situation had not happened, I would not have seen the real growth within myself. My intention was never to make her feel bad about her remark, it was just to state that I didn't like something, but somehow, I have caused her to see me as a different person, probably a person she thought she knew. It's unfortunate that two good-hearted people could mean well for each other and still end up hurting each other unintentionally.

The third incident that allowed me to see my real and true strength was when a very close friend asked me for a favour. After delivering the service and making a completely harmless comment, she took it as an offence. I refused to listen to what was so offensive to her because I saw it as childish. I think I got tired of always justifying myself. I also think she got tired of my behaviour. I think what caught me off-guard was a disrespectful text I got in return for not listening to her feelings. I decided to let go, and I believe that she also decided to let go. I knew within myself she wouldn't come back to make it right and I had already mastered not returning to friendship.

If a friend didn't see me as worthy enough to come to me to sort things out, then why am I putting extra strain on my heart, when they are sleeping comfortably in their bed? Again, another disagreement that maybe could have been avoided, but I think, like any relationship, things build up after a while and it can make it easier to walk away. This incident was a real wake-up call to the kind of path I wanted to have when it comes to having friends.

Overall, I never saw any of my ex-friends as bad or as people who betrayed me in any way. I will always see the good inside of them and remember the good times we shared.

You must allow yourself to see people for who they truly are, especially when it comes to petty stuff. Do not allow one unpleasant experience to see them as completely bad and then create enemies. No need to burden your heart with things that can be forgiven. If you can allow yourself to be associated with someone, find the space in your heart to give yourself the opportunity to feel free. After all, that friend was once someone you connected with and shared a piece of your life with.

I am not perfect, and I accept that I have hurt some of my friends along the line. It bothers me a bit, but that was never my intention. My intention is always to do good; I would never intend to bring hurt to anybody, but I realise that having good intentions can hurt too. Sometimes we can be passionate about something and mean someone well, but the way it comes across may have hurt them.

Enough about my lifetime of disagreements, we are here to talk about betrayal. What is betrayal? Betrayal is when someone you trust lies to you, cheats on you, abuses you or hurts you by putting their own self-interest first. I think we can all relate to feeling betrayed by someone we love or loved.

The question is, the person who did the betrayal, did they self-reflect to see where they went wrong and apologise? Some people have a problem with apologising when they have hurt someone. Are you that person? If you are, I challenge you to seek into yourself and see if you find it difficult to say three simple words, I AM SORRY! If this is something you struggle with, then this is an area in your life that you need to acknowledge and improve. I believe often people struggle to apologise because of pride, but research has proven that people find this challenging because it reflects their efforts to protect a fragile sense of self.

Some people do not understand how to separate their actions from their character, and if they did something bad, that means that they are a bad person. Apologising represents a major threat to their basic sense of identity. Some may also refuse to open the doors of guilt; they refuse to get in tune with their emotions or feel ashamed. Depending on the person, there could be various reasons why people may refuse to apologise. If you cannot see wrong in what you did, then you will fail to grow as an individual because you are not learning from your mistakes. You cannot expect others to apologise for their wrongs when you can't.

The saddest thing about betrayal is that it never comes from your enemies. It's always the person that is closest to you. I cannot compare the feeling of losing a friend through a disagreement to the feeling of betrayal. Some people have been through serious betrayals, and to write about this topic, I had to ask the public for their testimonies. So, get ready to read about real, true betrayal stories that may seem unforgivable.

## *Story No. 1*

One person confessed that she had a friend who refused to work and refused to be open to progression. She always tried to encourage her to do more so that she can see her true potential. She explained that probably the person wasn't on the same level as her. I applaud her for trying to motivate her friend to do more with her life. As a friend, I believe we have an obligation to encourage our friends to excel in life.

The person said that one day, the friend asked her for 60 dollars to buy an item for her house. She then explained to her friend that this was not important, and if she had wanted the money for an emergency, she would be happy to help, but she needed the money herself to get her through the rest of the week. The friend seemed to understand. Then on the weekend, they went out to a party, and while dancing, she handed over her purse to her friend. During the party, she decided to open her purse and then realised 60 dollars was missing. She explained that her initial thoughts were that the money fell out of her purse when she opened it to get her phone. She then told her friend, and they began to look for the money. Eventually, they gave up and concluded that the money was lost.

Another incident happened where the friend had taken a photograph, and she saw a bracelet on her hand that looked exactly like a bracelet she recently bought. She still didn't think anything about the situation and complimented the friend on how nice her bracelet looked. The friend thanked her and told her that her boyfriend bought it for her. One day, she decided to wear the bracelet for the very first time, and it was nowhere to be found. It then hit her that the friend that she loved was stealing from her. She explained that she never confronted the friend, she just drifted away. She said she felt so hurt and disappointed, but she blames herself in the sense that she picked a friend that wasn't ambitious. But how could she have known?

## *Story No. 2*

Imagine being in a happy relationship with your husband. Then three years after you get married, you receive a call from a friend stating that she has a confession to make. The friend confessed that she had an affair with her last partner behind her back. The person said when her friend told her this, she truly didn't know how to feel, because they were not as close as before and she had already moved on with her life. The question remains, why did the friend wait so long to confess? Could it be because she was jealous that she moved on and was happily married and she wanted to hurt her, or could it be because her conscience was killing her?

## *Story No. 3*

Social media has become such a big thing in today's society, and it can be used to embarrass others, which I class as a premeditated and spiteful act. This person explained that she'd had a friend for over five years, and it came to a point where the friend began to get very clingy. She was always attentive and wanted her to come by her house on a regular basis to cook and eat together. At some point, it started to become annoying.

One day she invited her over, and she wasn't in the mood and just wanted to chill with her boyfriend – the same boyfriend this friend tried to discourage her from being with. She decided to make up a lie and explained that she was low on funds. The friend then remarked, "What are doing with a man that cannot take care of you?" She immediately got offended, and they had an argument. The next day she received a call stating that this friend had written horrible things on Facebook about her.

The comment that confused me was, how could the friend state that she was always hungry, and she had to feed her like she was a stray dog? How could she make such a remark when she was the one inviting her over? The person said she felt complete betrayal because not only had the person lied about her, but they had years of friendship. She couldn't believe that a friend she ate, laughed, and drank with would do something so malicious. I think it is reasonable to ask why the person was dishonest with her friend? Why didn't she tell her friend that she was not in the mood? Maybe she didn't want to offend her.

## Story No. 4

Imagine having a best friend, and when you finally found a boyfriend, the true side of the friend came out. This person had a best friend, and she didn't understand why she always got angry and stormed out when her boyfriend came by. She said it took her a while to notice the behaviour, but she still never thought anything of it. They continued the friendship until one day her boyfriend was using the computer and she saw them saying I love you to each other. She immediately got angry and was hurt about it, but she wanted to understand what was going on. She then asked him if they were in a relationship. He confessed and said they'd had two affairs. The boyfriend told her best friend that she knew about the affair. She tried to call her best friend to see what her side of the story was, but she refused to talk to her and said she'd heard she had been saying bad things about her. She explained she never discussed the issue with anyone other than her boyfriend. She decided to give her boyfriend a second chance, and it didn't work out for other personal reasons. The friend then called her and asked her if it was okay to date her ex-boyfriend. She told her yes, but she felt completely betrayed.

She confessed that there were signs of jealousy, but when everything happened, it all started to make sense to her. She explained that the friend used to stuff her bra and hips with tissue so that she could look more appealing to men. After reminiscing about the past, she realised the friend was competing with her.

When we meet people and class them as a friend, we do not prepare our heart for betrayal. I gave four examples of betrayal, and there might be worse scenarios, but they all had something in common – pain and hurt, which led to a broken heart. You may even pose the question of why people betray people they said they loved. It could be because of jealousy, greed, power and fear. These reasons can push people to do dreadful things, which can cause unforgettable pain.

Why does betrayal hurt so much? Trust is the main foundation in any relationship, and when you trust someone you love or care for, you expect the person to feel the same way about you. It hurts because it's something that you weren't expecting, and it's hard for your brain to come to terms with what the person did. Your heart is the most fragile part of the body, and it feels like the person took a knife and stabbed you a thousand times. Your feelings are linked to your heart, and when someone causes you pain, it causes a heartache.

Can betrayal really be forgiven? Forgiveness will be discussed in the next chapter. Stay tuned to see if these women ever forgave their friends for betraying them.

The effects of betrayal can create trust issues for the future, damage self-esteem, create anger, hate, stress and anxiety, and can cause you to be an unforgiving person.

There are many more effects of betrayal, these are just a few, and everything listed affects the body and mind. If you betrayed someone, take a moment to think about how you made the person feel. We all make mistakes, and the most important thing is to forgive yourself, even if a friend hasn't forgiven you.

# Chapter 7
# Forgiveness

Can betrayal be forgiven? Some will say yes, and some will say no. Forgiveness is not for the person, it's for you to be free. Forgiving someone is a choice, so you choose whether you want to or not. Depending on the situation, forgiveness might seem like a very hard process.

Some people struggle with forgiveness for various reasons, and I like to be understanding and respectful, I am not here to pass judgement. I can only advise you to try and implement forgiveness in your life. I think it's natural for someone to express hurt and anger in their own way, and we must acknowledge that we are all human and we have blood running through our veins, but there must be a time where we **let go.** I guess some may pose the question of how? First, you need to know this.

Forgiveness *doesn't* mean:

- That you must be friends with the person again
- That you must let them know you have forgiven them
- That you must say hello to the person when you see them
- That you must forget what the person did to you
- That you are letting the person get away with it
- That you are justifying their actions
- That you are pretending that it never happened
- That you have to forgive someone instantly
- That you are weak
- Or that you are burying your pain six feet under

There are hidden scars that you will always remember, but you will no longer be bound by them. What is forgiveness? Forgiveness, as defined in Wikipedia, means the **intentional** and **voluntary process** by which someone undergoes a **change** in **feelings** and **attitude** regarding an offence and overcomes negative emotions such as resentment and vengeance. As you can see, this is a process, and everyone will have a different timescale for this process. It should not be forced! It is a voluntary process meaning choice, and you can go through this process whenever you are ready. It is intentional, meaning that you had to premeditate before making that decision. This change in feeling and attitude regarding the issue will be the opposite to what you feel about the person. No more resentment, anger, vengeance, sadness or hurt.

Remember, it takes a whole lot of effort and energy to carry a burden of hurt in your heart. Holding on to anger and hurt can weigh you down and have an impact on your health, happiness, and other relationships you may encounter. You might think it's easy; that's because you cannot see inside your body and see the effects.

It's okay to feel hurt and acknowledge these feelings because it is real, and it's okay if you are not ready to forgive someone. What's not healthy is holding on for several years. Forgiveness is not a feeling, and it's not about the past, it's about the future. I think learning to forgive with ease comes with growth and experience.

Forgiveness is not when you see your ex-friend, and you suddenly feel that sense of hurt that replays in your head and you get angry all over again. Forgiveness is not when you see that ex-friend and give them a bad look, and you wish that one look could kill them. Please note that this is *not* forgiveness!

How would you know that you have forgiven someone? Forgiveness is when you see that person who has done you wrong and feel a sense of relief, and you wish them all the best in life. It's not about keeping score, or feeling a sense of *we are even, now you know how that feels.* There should be no urge for revenge in your heart.

If you are struggling with forgiveness, you must first ask yourself, "Do I want to forgive the person who has wronged me?" If the answer is no, then do not force it, it should come naturally. I would advise that you find a way to concentrate on self-growth and happiness.

If yes, then you are a step closer to taking your power back. I would like to welcome you to the process of healing. Forgiveness is a healing process, and it allows you to feel better from within. Forgiveness is the final key to the puzzle of your life. It forces you to reflect and do some self-evaluation. Forgiveness forces you to familiarise yourself with your thoughts, feelings and boundaries.

Did the friends from the betrayal testimonies find it in their heart to forgive their ex-friends? Let's have a look!

The person who stole from her friend: the friend chose to forgive, and they are now mutual friends. Some might find it hard to believe, but forgiveness is a choice, and she showed great power by not allowing this hurt to consume her heart.

The ex-friend whose friend slept with her ex-boyfriend on numerous occasions: the friend decided to forgive her, but she explained when it comes to her husband, she is extremely cautious and no longer trusts people.

The ex-friend that slandered her friend's name on social media: the person explained that she cannot forgive her, and by the looks she had given her previously, she knew she hasn't forgiven her either. This is a choice; perhaps, over time, she will forgive her, who knows?

The friend who stuffed her bra and hips with tissues: the person forgave her and expressed how important it is to implement forgiveness.

It is understood that some forms of betrayal are unforgivable, for example messing with a person's child, trying to sabotage a person's marriage or disrespecting their parents. Some may agree, and some will disagree, but I get why it might seem impossible to implement forgiveness. I admit these are examples of serious betrayals that hurt and can take years to start to implement forgiveness.

There is one person in my life when growing up that I thought I would never be able to forgive. That was my dad, and I know the book is about friendship, but this is the only example in my life where I struggle with forgiveness. I was 22 years old when I made that choice to forgive him. I learnt full forgiveness when I gave my life to God. The hurt I felt went so deep into my heart that to get over this, I had to fully identify this hurt. I expressed to God how I felt, I cried out my anger and pain to him. Some of you might not be spiritual, and I respect that. However, you can find someone you trust to express these feelings to or just express them on paper or say them in the open air privately to yourself. To forgive, you must acknowledge the reality of what occurred and how you were affected.

In the process of forgiveness, try to find the growth and positivity out of the scenario. For example, what have you learnt about yourself or your life? How have you grown?

In the situation with my dad, I learnt that even though he wasn't there for me consistently as a father, I turned out awesome. I have grown into a beautiful, strong, independent young lady who knows exactly what she wants. I also realised this gave me the strength not to take any nonsense from men, and to know my value and my worth. I acknowledge that this situation made me and did not break me. Anything we go through in life that seems problematic can make us stronger.

I then evaluated him as a person and acknowledged that he is only human, and he made a mistake. I didn't need an apology to forgive him. Sometimes, we expect an apology before we can forgive, but we should try to forgive even if that's not the case because it's for our wellbeing. I told myself, one day he will come to a realisation. I don't think that he is a bad person, or he intentionally wanted to hurt me, but sometimes people do not realise their actions can affect others.

After I analysed all these aspects, I knew within my heart I had forgiven him because I felt so free – like a burden had been lifted off my shoulders. I could talk to him without expressing any anger. It took so much effort to show him how angry I was with him. Seeing and talking to him became effortless. I chose to forgive him. I took the power back.

Take that power back, don't allow anyone to make you bitter or allow you to feel sad or hurt. When you forgive, you heal, and when you let go, you grow.

For those of you who are Christians, I would like to offer a quote as a reminder: **Ephesians 4: 31-32. 31.** 'Let all bitterness, and wrath and anger and clamour, and evil speaking, be put away from you, with all malice: **32.** And be ye kind one to another, tender-hearted, forgiving one another, even as God for Christ's sake hath forgiven you.'

Remember this is a process and it will take time!

# Chapter 8
# Types of Friends

Can a bad quality in a friend define who they truly are? I tend not to see people for their bad qualities, I try to see people based on their heart, but how can you see someone's heart? Is it based on the things that they do or their personality?

It is said that you can see a man's face, but we can't see his heart. Sometimes people do great things, and we say they have a good heart, but deep down inside, they don't, and then years down the line you say you didn't know that person had bad intentions towards you. Could there be signs that we tend not to see, because we are trying to maintain the friendship, or could the person be a good pretender? From experience, I do believe some people can do great things and still have a good heart, but how do we pick that right one? Truth be told, it's all a gamble, we choose our friends based on experience, some of us might be naive like me for a very long time, but you will learn as you go along.

Often a bad quality can define a person. If we experience a betrayal from a friend, it is important that we try to learn from our experience by protecting our hearts. For example, the person in the previous chapter who had a friend who was stealing from her. She drifted away from that person, and she confessed that when she meets new people, she keeps them at arm's length. Then again, how could she have known that the friend she cared for and loved would steal from her? She couldn't and that's the thing, when we meet someone, they are strangers and as time goes by, we build a relationship with the person. A bad experience can ruin a person's behaviour and approach to genuine people.

There is a saying, 'one bad apple spoils the bunch', but people aren't apples. Don't let the poor choices of one person spoil the way you feel about others. Easier said than done, right? I agree. I can't follow this saying, and I am not going to act like I am a saint, because I am not. One bad apple has spoiled it for others because I must protect my heart. Even though I haven't experienced betrayal, I still have a sense of sadness for every friend/sister that I have lost.

Our friends can have good qualities that we should appreciate, but the question remains, 'Are friends with bad qualities worth your lifetime of friendship?' I listed a few types of friends that we may have experienced in the past or are currently experiencing.

- The controlling friend
- The inspirational friend
- The supportive/helpful friend
- The user
- The jealous friend
- The loud friend
- The selfish friend
- The judgemental friend
- The delusional friend
- The acquaintance
- The childish friend
- The friend who always has an excuse
- The friend who is never motivated
- The angry friend
- The comparing friend
- The boastful friend
- The favour friend
- The ungrateful friend
- The complaining friend
- The uptight friend

- The petty friend
- The depressed friend
- The insecure friend
- The friend that has high expectations
- The spiritual friend

I know I haven't touched on all types of friends and there may be other types that you have experienced. But I am sure while you were reading, you have had flashbacks, or you agreed to the points due to your experience. Every person thinks that they are a good friend, I have never met anyone who saw themselves as a bad friend. Have you?

There is good and bad in everyone no matter what type of friend they are. There is good and bad in me, and I take it upon myself to reflect and work on the ugly side of me.

## *The users*

I have experienced people in my life who have used me because they know I am always willing, and I can't say no. Saying no to someone would make me feel like I was disappointing them. By the way, this is not the right mindset to have in any relationship. I have also had people in my life that only call when they need a favour. The important question to ask yourself is, 'Are they your true friend or are they just using you because they know you are willing?'

When I turned 25, I learnt that I should not allow people to use me, and it is okay to say no. I think it took me a long time to wake up, but I applaud myself for learning to say no. Eventually, I got tired of people using me, and when I started to say no, they began to get upset and say I was not a good friend because I couldn't be there for them at that particular time. Things like this saddened my heart because I wondered if they had forgotten when I made myself available to help them in the past. It puzzles me that people have these mindsets. Always remember you cannot please people all the time. At the age of 25, I was finding my path in friendship.

If you have a friend that gets upset with you or curses you for not being able to be there for them for whatever reason, and in your heart you know you are a supportive friend, then this is not someone you want to keep in your life. Their expectations from you are too high and cannot be met. Your friend should know that if you cannot be available, you genuinely cannot be available. You should also be able to give your friend a reasonable explanation as to why you cannot be available, and it should be respected. Don't allow anyone to change your personality because they used you, without a care in the world. Do not give the users the satisfaction of ruining it for good people who need genuine help. It's always good to do good, I believe when you do good, good is then returned to you somewhere along the way.

If you choose to be with a friend that you know uses you because you see the good in that person and you want to maintain the friendship, you could speak to them about their behaviour. However, that might not turn out very well, because not everyone is good at acknowledging their wrongdoing, and it might affect your friendship in the future. I would highly recommend that you slowly start saying no with a valid reason and building boundaries, perhaps that friend just got too comfortable and is now taking you for granted. It is especially important that you respect your friend's private life, you should not use and abuse them.

## *The ungrateful friend*

Have you ever had a friend where nothing you did was good enough? They keep wanting more and more, but still, in the end, they fail to see the good that you did for them. You have been there for them through thick and thin, and they still turn around and have the audacity to say you are not a good friend. Sometimes people do not realise how good a friend you were until you are gone; it is their loss, not yours. These are time-wasters who are unsure about what they want in life. They can also be classed as users because they have used you to get where they need to get in life and then disposed of you into the general waste bin.

## The supportive/helpful friend

I can honestly say I have always had friends who have consistently supported me, whether it's physically, financially, mentally, or emotionally. Whether we talk or not, I will remain forever appreciative of all their support and helping hands. That one bad experience won't define how I see them. After all, they were once my sister in my eyes.

I realised that I get on better with people who are much older than me. I currently have a friend who is in her fifties, and she has become more like family than a friend. She is someone I look up to. She is very talented with many skills, and I am positive that there is nothing she could not do (mechanics, builder, dressmaker, singer and the list goes on). I admire her talent.

This is a person I grew to love and appreciate, there was never a time that I called her, and she was not available. Whatever she did for me, I could see the joy in her face, just to give a helping hand. I think we are quite similar, but she is much kinder than I am. I believe our relationship works because she is much older, and she has been through so many experiences and chose a peaceful life. I call her the supportive friend; this friend is a keeper not for what she can do but for who she is.

## The acquaintance

I have had an associate that showed up for me more than someone I considered a sister. This situation always surprises me. How could someone you associate yourself with show up more than someone who is closer to you? Someone who barely knows you, cares enough to help in times of need. This proves that there are good people in this world, and I believe that people are placed in our lives for different reasons.

Acquaintances can become your friend because friendship is built over time. I immediately start trusting that acquaintance for that good thing they did for me, I start seeing them as a sister. This is not necessarily the right way to see things, and as I got older in my twenties, it all started to make sense to me. I need to give people time before letting them in my life. I needed time to learn about the person's character and see if it fits with my character. I needed time to trust. Luckily, this acquaintance is still one of my friends. She showed up when I had my firstborn and was incredibly supportive. She was always willing to go the extra mile when it came to childcare, which I would forever be thankful for.

What is the difference between an acquaintance and a friend? An acquaintance is a person known to you, but you rarely see each other. They are not obligated to help in times of need. A friend is someone who you share a strong bond with, who knows the most intimate details about you. They are the first person you call when you are in trouble or need advice. I admit I struggle to understand the difference between the two. Sometimes when someone is extremely kind to me, I tend to class them as a friend before giving myself enough time to know them properly.

Research has proven that it takes 50 hours spent with someone before you consider them a casual friend, 90 hours before you become real friends and 200 hours to become close friends. The shocking part about this research is that 200 hours is equivalent to eight days. Would you agree that this is not enough time to truly know someone before classing them as a close friend? The more I analyse my journey with friendship, I have to agree with the research statistics, but I would like to add that if someone has had a bad experience with friendship, the figure could increase to 438,000 hours, which is equivalent to 50 years.

There are four levels of friendship: stranger, acquaintance, close friend and best friend. Do not be swift to issue hall passes to strangers or acquaintances to become close or best friends, as holding onto the hall pass for up to a year might still not guarantee a lifetime of friendship.

## *The complaining friend*

The companion friend sees herself as the complaining friend. One day she asked me if I saw her as a person who always complains. The answer to that is no, not because she expresses the way she feels in a way that means that she could be labelled as a complaining friend. If I can't offer the free service of a listening ear, then why are we friends? I will never see her as the complaining friend because I'm supposed to be there for her no matter what. I know for some people, having a complaining friend might seem very annoying, but because I have a passion for people, I am open to being patient. I think my job is to help them come up with a solution to their problem. I think my crazy idea of having a sibling or a friend caused me to develop this trait. I will say I went away with a positive from this delusion.

When the companion friend and I talk, I feel like no judgements are passed. Yes, there have been times when we disagree, but in fairness, it was done with respect. Even through disagreements, she showed me that I am a friend worth having. It is not just me showing interest. We both know what we have, and when two people can show each other they are both valuable in each other's life then the friendship can work.

We have had 11 years' worth of friendship. I believe that it lasted this long, because we both think highly of each other. Have you ever had a friend and the way you saw them was slightly different from how they saw you? You may have classed them as a close friend while they classed you as an associate. This could hurt just thinking about it, but you can tell a lot by a person's actions. Evaluate your friend's actions and if you find yourself putting in more of the effort, then you need to assess how high you are scoring them as a friend."

If I had a disagreement with my ex-friends, it was always me running back to them apologising and trying to fix things to show how much I valued our friendship. It can hurt to see that they didn't care enough to even reach out. I often wonder if they didn't truly care about the years we had built. The least long-lasting relationship lasted for eight years, I have even lost a friendship that lasted for 11 years. I got tired of running back to fix the relationship, I got tired of breaking the ice. Some people can easily let go of people, and that is not necessarily a bad thing. If they decide to let go, it's because they value their peace and happiness more. I believe your happiness should always come first, and if someone is obstructing that in any way, I agree to cutting them loose, even if it's me that caused the grief.

## The loud friend

I have always been attracted to loud, outgoing people who I found exciting. I wasn't so much attracted to quiet people. I think it's because I am an only child and life was boring at home, so when I went out, I needed to be entertained. Sometimes a loud friend can be very embarrassing when you go out in public places. The older I got, the less attention I wanted.

## The inspirational friend

Do you know someone who knows exactly what they want, and they will do anything to ensure they get what they need? This is a fantastic quality to have as a person. I class these as the inspirational friends. They are always the one to encourage you to be a go-getter, and they use their life as living proof that anything is possible. These are people you want to keep close to you. They will always inspire you with different ideas to do different things. You do not want a friend that is not motivated to do anything and then is jealous of your success.

I have an inspirational friend, I met her at work when I was 23 years old. She lived in France at the time, but she came to the UK to do an internship at my company. She is also an only child, and the more we had lunch breaks together, the more we realised the positive impact we had on each other's lives. She is very career-orientated and knows exactly what she wants and isn't afraid to challenge herself to be successful. She always encourages me to do more for myself and reminds me of my potential. She sometimes gets annoyed with me when she sees I fear to strive for more. We do not see each other often, but we ensure we check on each other to see how life is. I always admire her bravery.

## The selfish friend

It is very hard to deal with someone who is all about themselves and only cares about their own wellbeing and won't go the extra mile to do anything for you, but still expects you to go the extra mile for them. For me, I cannot be around selfish people, and I would not advise anyone to be around someone so self-centred. Selfish people need to be around selfish people! I think they understand each other better, both will get a taste of their own medicine, and hopefully they can grow and evolve from the experience.

## A favour friend

The worst type of friend is a friend that does a favour in return for a favour. If you are not able to return the favour, they are the first to remind you when they were there for you. If you are going to help a friend, help a friend without keeping score. If you are keeping score, that means you didn't do it from your heart. Whatever you do, your right hand should not know what the left hand did. If you know someone who boasts about doing a favour for a friend, then this is a sign that they are a favour friend.

Sometimes when people do favours for us, we think that we are obligated to them for life. Never allow guilt to force you to maintain a toxic relationship. Always be true and genuine to yourself and others.

## The comparing friend

Comparing friends are friends that have a lot of insecurities. You will see them focusing on your life, and then minor things become an issue. They are so focused on looking up at you that they cannot take a moment to look down on themselves to see how they can better their lives.

Stay away from friends that are always comparing their lives with you openly. This is a sign that you are not compatible. Some people cannot stand to see their friends doing better than them, they prefer to see their friend beneath them. Bad traits always come to light because what is done in the dark will become known; meaning that the truth will eventually reveal itself.

## The boastful friend

Some people get great satisfaction when their friends are jealous of their lives. They will always go out of their way to boast about their lives to the person that they know shows jealous traits. These are two toxic people who are insecure and do not understand the value of life.

Boastful people always look for compliments from others to feel valued. They are known to be pretenders. They tend to believe that someone is always jealous of them because of how they look and what they have. They lack confidence and are trying to feel valued by behaving like they are more important than others. Ignore and avoid these kinds of people to prevent additional stress.

Is it sensible to discuss your success, when your friend is going through a difficult time? Can this also be classed as boasting? Should you wait for their situation to change, before sharing your good news? I believe that you should be compassionate and understanding towards your friend's situation, and then evaluate the right time to update them about your contentment. You might do this if a friend is experiencing a bereavement for example.

I also believe, that your friend should be able to congratulate you on your success despite their sad moments. Your friend may not truly express how happy they are, but if your friend is usually supportive, try to ignore their unusual lack of interest.

Some friends tend to see you as boasting because things are not working out for them as they would like. It takes a true and genuine friend to be there for others when their own world seem to be falling apart. We all have low moments, but they never last forever. Pick yourself up and believe that you can overcome any situation. Accepting negativity or failure should never be an option! Your struggles should never define who you are, but should form part of your journey to make you stronger. Where there is life, there is hope. You have the power to shape your future; no need for jealousy - start planning and creating what works best for you.

## *The jealous friend*

Years of friendship can eventually lead to jealousy. They might envy you based on your possessions, promising opportunities, success or good relationships. An observation I've made, is that jealous traits ultimately reveal themselves.

Signs that your friend might be jealous include:

- They look for something negative to say about your accomplishments.
- They do not offer support.
- They compete with you by trying to out-do you.
- They compare their lives with you openly.

- They pull away from you slowly or act tense when something significant is happening in your life.
- They're not interested in listening to you and then make it all about themselves.
- They struggle with insecurities, which allows them to carry jealous traits.
- They pretend to be happy for you with a plastic smile because your success makes them uncomfortable.
- Their facial expression changes; before congratulating you there may be a small silence or a moment of shock.
- They roll their eyes or make faces when you tell them about your good fortune.
- They constantly try to discourage you by saying the words, 'You can't!'
- They diminish everything you accomplish. For example, "Well that was easy. I could have done that."
- They would openly say, "I wish that was me."
- They try to mirror your life.
- They get upset when you socialise with other friends.

## *The petty friend*

What do you think of friends who expect you to have the same enemies? If they have an enemy, they expect you to also be enemies with the same person. Some people cannot cope with you befriending an enemy because they feel like you might talk about them to the person. Sometimes that is the case, but I think it is very childish to remain enemies with someone that didn't do you wrong. In general, people cannot be trusted, and if you have a friend that is going to a known enemy to use you as a round table talk, then this person is a wolf in sheep's clothing. If that person returns to you about something the enemy said about you, then this is a warning that they are discussing you, and your secrets are no longer secrets. As teenagers, we tend to keep the same enemies as our friends because we class it as loyalty. However, there comes a point in life where childish behaviours are put away.

In the Urban dictionary, 'petty' is defined as making things, events, or actions normal people dismiss as trivial or insignificant into excuses to be upset, uncooperative, childish, or stubborn. Someone who is petty seems to be on a mission to make you feel dejected because they will take a minor subject and blow it up, out of proportion. You will always be able to spot a petty person from a mile away, but we tend to ignore the signs for the sake of the friendship.

## *The friend who is not motivated*

Have you ever met up with an old friend and decided to have a conversation with them and you realised that they haven't changed or elevated themselves? They are still stuck in the exact same place you left them. Many people lack ambition, and I would advise you to look back and feel proud of yourself because you have grown past that situation. Your situation did not define who you are today. Thank them in your mind for assisting you to see a clearer path.

## *The depressed friend*

Do you have a friend who is always depressed? How frustrating! You might think to yourself, why is this person's life always sad, why are they always putting themselves in a box? It might be very hard for you to understand why, but everyone deals with things differently. I know that listening to their cycle of problems can be overwhelming, and they might suck the energy out of you. It's hard to walk away from a friend that needs emotional support, I would advise you to only be around that person when you can mentally and physically handle them. Advise them to seek professional help. I do not think you would be a true friend if you abandoned them because they are depressed.

What you need to understand is that this is a mood disorder that causes a persistent feeling of sadness and loss of interest. If something was to happen to this friend, you would feel guilty if you weren't there to support them.

## The delusional friend

Have you ever watched a friendship movie and then wished you had friends like the movie portrayed? The movie makes it looks so easy to sustain healthy friendships and that all parties appreciate each other and can work through any situation. I always try to find a character that suits who I am, and sometimes I sit there wishing I had something just like this. I would wish I had a group of friends, and we were all very close. Can you relate?

We have all experienced different types of friends, and after finding out about their personality, the choice is always yours if you want to continue the friendship or remain mutual. Frequently we ignore the bad signs in people and then question why it didn't work. Everyone has different tolerance levels; learn how to accept yours, so you do not allow any additional pressure or pain in your life.

# Chapter 9
# My Husband Is My Best Friend

My husband is more than just a partner, he is my best friend. It took me a while to acknowledge that my husband is my best friend and to learn to appreciate him as a friend and then a partner. I saw him as a friend, but I never really recognised and accepted that he is probably one of the greatest friends who has been placed in my life. Often, we use words loosely and do not acknowledge the true meaning of what we are saying.

How could I not acknowledge this? I believe, losing friends has allowed me to value my husband for what he truly is, 'my best friend'. Even before he became my husband, he was my boyfriend, who stood by me through thick and thin. It's only because we made the vows that he became my husband. But just like any relationship, having a husband is not guaranteed forever if both parties do not honour their vows. We might not be the perfect couple who get everything right, and like any relationship, we do have our roller-coaster rides. If there is one thing I am sure of, it is that God placed him in my life, so I will never have the feeling of loneliness again. We have been together a total of nine years, with five years of marriage. Shame on me that it took me this long to realise that 'my husband is my best friend'.

He is the type of person that remains present with anything I decide to do, he is always willing to support me. When I decided to start my own business, he helped me set it up and promote it. He even went to the extent of staying up late in the night to help me wrap the gift baskets. When I was studying to accomplish my health and safety qualification, every night he stayed up and encouraged me, saying, "You can do this," and tested my knowledge on the topic. No matter the circumstance, I can always count on him.

If I want to go shopping and I have no one to go with, I can ask him to come with me, even though he gets miserable after 30 minutes. He cares about my wellbeing, and when I am sad it makes him feel very uncomfortable, but he tries his best to make me happy. We are both comfortable to be ourselves, and we can make jokes and be goofy around each other. When I am sick, he is the person that is there to support me by bringing me a cup of tea or comforting me when needed.

He is the person that knows my every move and my every facial expression. He knows my favourite food, he knows my hobbies, my skills, and my abilities. This person knows me inside out.

Every morning I wake up with him beside me, and he makes me feel safe and secure. Travelling the world together is something we both have in common. We both enjoy the adventure of exploring the culture, food, and historical buildings.

He is the person I vent to about work or issues I might face with someone. He might not always give me the advice I want to hear, but he is honest, and he tries to comfort me, to let me know that everything will be okay. Sometimes he gets frustrated to hear me talk about the same thing over and over because I refuse to let it go. I can see it in his face that he tries to tolerate me because he has already advised me, but I will continue to vent, ignoring the look on his face. He is a friend that tolerates me regardless of my flaws.

There are so many signs that show that my husband is my best friend. I think I was too caught up in trying to maintain close friendships, instead of seeing what I am blessed with. He might not be a female friend, but a friend is a friend. At the age of 27, I finally woke up to what exactly was in front of me. I do believe we should have other friendships and relationships outside of marriage because if we didn't, I am sure we would drive each other crazy. It is not healthy not to have a social life. If you find that one partner has more of a social life than the other, then you need to start finding hobbies you like doing without them where you can meet new people. Trust me, not having outside friendships can put a serious strain on the relationship because you then depend on this person to meet your every need as a friend, partner and even a dad, and when he is not available, you might feel like you are all alone. Would you agree that, this is a lot of pressure and expectation to put on one person, even though your partner should meet your every need?"

How many of us can say our partner is our best friend? Think about it, married or not, if you are in a relationship with someone, you have to become friends before you become partners. They consume your personal space even when you can't stand them to be around.

See your husband as a friend before you see them as a partner. When you are in a marriage or a serious relationship, your partner should automatically become your best friend. This may have an impact on your prior friends, but they should always be the person you turn to first for anything. Building a friendship with your partner helps to sustain a healthy and long-lasting relationship. At times he might not show the qualities of a good friend and may disappoint you, but he is only human. If he is trying to be a good husband or friend, then the relationship or friendship is worth pursuing.

I think my husband is my opposite, and that makes our friendship and relationship work. For example, he is the listener and I am the talker. He is not a very talkative person, but I always ensure I give him my undivided attention to encourage him that he can talk to me about anything.

When I think about my husband and me, I have no time to be grieving over disagreements, I need to utilise my time on my marriage and my family. That alone is enough work to sustain and maintain. Any additional stress I refuse to add to my list. Going forward, I will always choose a happy and healthy relationship!

# Chapter 10
# Self-Evaluation

Self-evaluation is a process that allows us to reflect on ourselves. To do this, we must go deep within our soul, to pull all the good and bad out. Sometimes it's hard to evaluate ourselves, but we must remember that no one is perfect. It's easier to look at another man's fault than it is to evaluate your own. In any bad or confrontational situation, wrong or right, I always ask myself, **what could I have done differently?**

I sometimes believe that if people did a lot of self-evaluation, relationships would last longer. Taking accountability for your actions is important.

Making excuses, playing the victim or putting the blame on another person is not taking full accountability for your actions. When you are taking accountability for your actions, there is no *sorry* and then a *but*. Forget the *but*. It's *I am sorry for what I did* full stop. Taking accountability for your actions is a strength, you are taking ownership of your thoughts, behaviour, actions, and performance. Saying sorry is not weakness, it's growth! Do not let pride hold you back from being the best person you can be.

Being wrong, or someone telling you something about your flaws, might not feel good, but it can be true and is often hard for an individual to accept. Even though we may not like to be corrected or for someone to show us our flaws, we must be able to look back and take a moment and try to understand what the person is saying. Our friends are meant to be honest with us to help us to improve ourselves. I do believe it is not what you say, but it is how you say it.

Yes, sometimes people say stuff that you may not agree with a hundred percent, but they are entitled to their own opinions. An opinion is a view or judgement formed about something, not necessarily based on fact or knowledge. So why should you allow yourself to feel offended by an opinion? If there is one thing I have learnt through my path of friendship, it is that someone's words do not define who I am. People are free to say whatever they like, and we shouldn't give them the power to control our emotions. I admit in the past, I struggled to ignore people's comments, and at times people took control of my emotions, but over the years, I have seen growth within myself. People's comments are becoming more irrelevant to me because I choose to take power over my feelings. I have the power to dismiss someone's opinion because it's not based on facts. I realised that people tend to make negative comments based on their own insecurities.

I know there are so many different people in this world with different values and a different outlook on life, but always remain true to who you are. Some people can be difficult, but this chapter is not about other people, it's about self-evaluation.

Although I class myself as a good friend, I know there are things within me that my friends must put up with. There are also things within my friends that I must put up with. We all must put up with something, but which friends are worth it? Having negative flaws doesn't mean you are a bad person; it means that you are human.

Within my path of friendship, I was able to acknowledge my flaws, and I made a choice to work on them. I might not get it right all the time, but my flaws can affect my current and future relationships.

Here is a list of my flaws.

1. When I lose my temper, I find it very hard to talk in a calm manner, and this applies in any confrontational situation.

2. I am very sensitive to words, and I can easily be offended if something is not said in the right way. I dislike being around people who use their words carelessly without thinking before they talk.
3. When I know I am right, I am right!
4. I may not always express how I truly feel if I think it's going to start an argument. Sometimes, things may build up, and then I explode like a volcano.
5. I am always assuming what someone is thinking.
6. Sometimes if someone does not understand my point, I will not shut up until they do – I do not like to be misinterpreted.
7. Most times I think very little of myself and I do not give myself credit when it's due.

I can remember two occasions when I completely lost it at my friends because I felt that one wasn't supportive during my life-changing event, and one provoked me with her words when I asked her to stop challenging me over and over again.

Once I lose it, I can become horrendous. I find myself shouting and cursing; this is something I hate about myself. I think I behave like this because I feel like I am in the right. When it comes to an actual confrontation, I get angry and a side of me will come out that I hate to see. I often try to self-reflect and question why I can't speak calmly in a challenging situation. Do you think it has something to do with my childhood, or is it's just who I am? Whatever it is, I choose to eliminate this flaw that causes me to look ugly and cause hurt.

After becoming vulgar with my friends, and I take a moment to calm down, I cry about my behaviour, and then a spirit of disappointment will come over me. I cannot live with myself, knowing that I talked to someone so horribly because I was angry. I accept that I was wrong by apologising many times, and I will try to make things right in numerous ways (flowers, chocolate, whatever it takes). If they decide not to deal with me after my bad behaviour, I will accept it, because there is no just reason for my actions. Have you ever heard that two wrongs don't make a right? I cannot continue to shy away from confrontational situations because I would continue to struggle on how to gain full self-control. I must come to term with my fear and learn how to express myself in a calm and respectable manner.

I had to learn to control myself and learn to walk away, I might not always get it right, but acknowledging this is a step to change. I am still learning how I can truly control my emotions. I will never accept the ugliness within me or not allow myself to change. You might be wondering how? I try not to express myself when I'm angry and I will try to talk about it later. This will allow me to formulate my thoughts thoroughly and efficiently. If things get heated, I remind myself that the person's words have no power over my emotions. If I continue to feel aggravated, I will take a moment to pause or walk away. I have full control of my emotions and I acknowledge that not everything requires a reaction. If I fail to comply, then I'll write a new plan on how to control myself effectively. If you have a friend that continuously brings the worst out of you, then maybe you need to analyse yourself and your friend, and consider the effectiveness of the friendship.

When you hear someone say I am who I am, and I refuse to change to please society, they are just scared to lose power. But what they don't know is that they have lost power by not allowing their hearts to open up to start the process of change. They fail to see that there is power when you can say, "I used to be like that, but I am no longer that person." When you can look back on your life and see the growth in yourself, it's one of the greatest accomplishments ever, it's like winning a marathon.

I was told by an ex-friend that she doesn't feel comfortable to talk to me about my flaws. For me, I can respect her opinion, but I will not accept I am like that. I have been known to act as if I am more important than others. I have two options, either allow the comment to define who I am or let it go. Sometimes people see you completely different to who you really are. You do not have to accept every negative thing about yourself. If a person said something you didn't agree with, say okay, look into yourself, and if you honestly do not feel that way, let it go!

When I lost two close friends in less than three months, I wondered if I was the problem. Maybe I was, maybe I wasn't, finding your path in friendship is all about self-growth and ownership of your actions that can help you to be a better person. We cannot act as if we have never hurt a friend whether it was them who hurt you first or you who hurt them first. We are only humans.

I challenge you to write three bad flaws about yourself below.

Flaws

1. _____
   _____
   _____

2. _____
   _____
   _____

3. _____
   _____
   _____

Then just ask yourself, are these flaws allowing me to be the best person I can be? Can these flaws affect my current friendships or relationships? **What can I do differently** to eliminate or reduce these bad habits from coming to light? Take a moment to reflect, you might not be able to figure it out right now, and that's okay, just remember to always practice self-reflection when a tough situation arises. The big question is,

**What can I do differently?** Keep asking yourself **how** until you cannot think of another solution. The best way to complete this activity, is by writing it down on paper so your thoughts can formulate effectively and efficiently.

Now write five positives about yourself.

Positives

1. _____

2. _____

3. _____

4. _____

5. _____

I purposely ended with the positive because I wanted you to leave this chapter feeling great about yourself!

Sometimes when we say things, we start to believe the words, and then our actions start to play out what we believe. Our words have a power that we may not even be aware of.

Always speak positive words to yourself, even when you wake up, tell yourself that you are beautiful and worthy. It is the start of having a wonderful day because those words that you used as an affirmation are then released into the atmosphere for a better day.

# Chapter 11
# How to Treat a Friend

Some people may not know the true meaning of friendship and how to treat a friend. Sometimes it has nothing to do with them, but their lifestyle (how they grew up and what they saw). Some people are terrible friends and don't even realise it. The fact is, if you have a terrible friend, probably it's time to start putting in boundaries and knowing what you want in your life. Like anything in life, we must make wise choices.

Treat people the way you would like to be treated or do unto others as you would wish them to do unto you. This is my number one rule on how to treat a friend. Your friend should always be treated with love and respect.

If you have a friend that values you and shows you that you are meaningful to them, never let a disagreement break that friendship, especially if it can be sorted. If you have a disagreement, just take a couple days out to calm down and reflect about your actions or what you said and then sort it amongst yourselves. Venting to the wrong friend about the disagreement can make it worse. From experience, disagreeing with a friend over things that are always being misinterpreted can be very draining and eventually you get tired of the same cycle.

When your friend is down, you should be able to enlighten them by making them feel a little better about themselves. Friends should never discourage each other but always encourage each other to reach for the stars. You should be able to support your friends in times of need and console them during challenging times.

# FINDING YOUR PATH IN FRIENDSHIP

I do not believe that you should completely stop talking to someone you once called your friend, but that's my opinion. Some have said, I am too lenient. Some people can stop talking to their ex-friends and treat them like complete enemies or strangers because of hurt. This is logical because we all deal with things differently. When I greet an ex-friend, I feel relieved just to say "hi". It makes me feel very uncomfortable to see someone I know and not say hello. Don't get me wrong if I said hello to someone and they blanked me, this action would not be repeated. I think I have a very weird passion for people. I love to treat people well and seeing them happy makes me happy. I have not allowed my bad experiences to change my personality, but I use my experience as a learning tool for finding my path in friendship.

How long can it take for a friend to feel comfortable to say hi to an ex-friend? Two years, five years, ten years, or a lifetime? Some people can hold on to things for life, but for some, after a couple years have passed, it feels childish not to say hello.

Years of friendship can allow you to master the action of tiptoeing around a friend because your words may cause offence. You should be able to walk freely but also respectfully. If you are tiptoeing to hypothetically prevent a cut from a glass, then that shows that you are not likeminded; you should always feel free in any relationship. We all make mistakes, and acknowledging when we are wrong to the person we call our friend is especially important. I believe it shows the person how much you value them as a friend.

There are still quite a few people that know how to treat a friend. Some people still know the value and loyalty of friendship. I think we must go through ups and downs with friends so we can learn about ourselves and others.

We all want someone to be there for us to support us. We are all looking for a genuine friend. The key to being a good friend is to be genuine. Genuine means: 'truly what something is said to be; authentic, or a person, emotion, or action that is sincere'.

# Chapter 12
# Letting Go

I had to finally let go of holding on to friendships like my life was on the line. I decided to let go, not because I didn't see the value of friends, but because I realised I was putting others before myself. I often wondered if I valued other people more than myself. If you have a weird personality disorder like me, the best option is to keep fewer friends. Letting go allowed me to see my blessings, I am alive, I have a beautiful family and a handful of friends.

I had to let go of the dream of always wanting a sister and the need to try to fill the gap of being alone. This childish behaviour could no longer continue if I wanted to be the best person I could be.

The more I learnt about letting go, the more I learnt how to keep certain aspects of my life to myself. I think I am a vulnerable person who is very open about my life. I have always seen this as being honest to help others. I must confess that I hate this quality in myself.

Letting go wasn't easy, but when you are persistent about a change, it becomes easier. If no one sees the value of me being their friend that is okay, because I finally saw the light. They must also do what is best for them.

I can remember when I was 20 years old and I had a disagreement with a friend, who today I can again call my sister. It took me many weeks to get over it and every night I went to bed thinking about it. I would even role-play and try to reinvent the situation differently; talking it through with myself, whether walking to the bus stop or washing the dishes, and I realized that this was consuming my thoughts. I hated this obsessive and possessive behaviour and I believe I carried this trait because I refused to let go and did not have the maturity yet to comprehend.

Twenty-seven was the golden age when I no longer had sleepless nights or talked to myself like I was going crazy when a situation occurred in my friendship. I finally learnt how to let go, this was the greatest feeling ever. Letting go showed that I was growing and developing and finding my path in friendship.

It's okay to let go of the toxic people in your life, I do not think my ex-friends were deliberately toxic, it was just not meant to be. I guess this is where it shows that people may only be in your life for a season. Sometimes things happen between you and your friends, and you may not understand what went wrong, do not beat yourself up about it. Use some of the points in my journey to help you get through. Always try to find the positive in any situation, for example, I am a stronger person, I am happier, or I am free. People coming in and out of your life is a confirmation that this is the cycle of life.

Sometimes people go through situations where they do not understand how to control their emotions or behaviour towards others. Don't try to find fault in yourself like I did, because you will end up trying to please people that can only change if they decide to. I think people-pleasers often feed themselves with negative self-talk, and pleasing others makes them feel valued in life. I often believe that you attract toxic people when you carry good traits.

Here is the process I followed to help me find my path in friendship.

- Forgiveness
- Self-evaluation
- Letting go
- Realisation
- Adjusting and accepting

I don't want anyone to have high expectations of me, because I am not someone that looks for high expectations from others. All I expect is a listening ear and a word of encouragement. I wanted to be free with myself and finally enjoy being an only child. I first had to learn to enjoy my own company. Sometimes we need to isolate ourselves from the world to just have a moment of silence to reflect.

I wanted to be free like a bird, free from the crazy stuff that I thought was friendship. I thought friendship should be long-lasting, but life has proven that it's never guaranteed.

Letting go of a friend is a challenging decision, some people can let go without even thinking of the good and bad of the person. I think it's important to try and sustain a long-lasting friendship so that you are not jumping from friend to friend. I also think it's important we try to maintain stable relationships because it is a long process to learn about someone and adapt to who they are and vice-versa. The older I got, the less interest I had in trying to meet people and classing them as a friend. I was no longer interested in having a sisterly bond with anybody.

Some people may find it very hard to sustain long-lasting friendships, and there could be various reasons why. Perhaps you're a person that is trying to guard your heart, or things might be happening in your life that you haven't figured out yet.

When you are letting go of friendship for whatever reason, it should be for your peace of mind and happiness. You might miss the good times you and the person shared, but just like anything in life, you learn to adjust and adapt.

You should not have to feel like you are in a cage when you are in a friendship. You are not obligated to anyone for the good they did for you. You should always be grateful and show gratitude, but you should never feel like you are sustaining a friendship because of the good deeds the person did. Think about it, you didn't force them to do it, they were supposed to do it from their hearts and because they love you, if some reason they choose to remind you by dangling it in front of your face, then that shows that they were not a true friend in the first place. Sometimes our mind tells us that we are obligated even when deep down within our hearts we know the person is toxic. The mind is a powerful weapon, you can invent, create, experience and destroy with just a thought. We tend to listen to our mind before we listen to our hearts.

Have you ever questioned yourself, as to why it's easier to let go of an actual friend rather than a partner? Would you consider the fact, that you might be connected on a deeper level i.e. intimacy, which allows you to be more forgiving and understanding? Or should we just accept that it's a complicated topic to explore?

Let go of people who are always disappointing you, are jealous of you, who criticise you, who play the victim, who bring negative energy, who waste your time, who use you, who add no value to your life and who are self-centred. If the relationship is toxic, let it go because you are only poisoning yourself.

# Chapter 13
# The Realisation

Like anything in life, there comes a point when we must wake up and smell the coffee. At the age of 27, I finally woke up, and I knew exactly what I wanted in life. I found what worked and what didn't work for me.

What worked for me was keeping my friends at a distance and not being in their space 24/7. As I got older, I didn't have time to be in people's personal space. Visiting friends occasionally and giving a helping hand when needed is what I wanted to do going forward. I always enjoy giving a helping hand to people in times of need, without any strings attached. I take no joy in watching someone struggle if I can help. This is a trait I choose to keep within my personality, no matter how bad an experience I may have.

I hated the fact that the people that I was close to knew so much about my life and all my secrets, and now it's over. I don't know why that bothered me so much, I guess it was because I was afraid that they might tell my secrets to their other friends and they were my secrets to tell. Every friend has a friend that they can trust, but I choose to stop introducing people into my life and learned how to keep certain aspects of my life private

I can finally understand the person's concept at the beginning of the chapter, although my experience wasn't betrayal, I just got tired of trying to maintain friendships, and despite my time and effort, I still lost them.

If I have to struggle to maintain a friendship, I'd rather be by myself in this world without a friend. I agree that friendship works best at a distance. At last, her theory finally made sense and the more I practiced it, the more I felt relaxed and released.

My biggest regret is that as a teenager, I took my mom for granted, and I didn't realise all this when, in fact, my mom was my true best friend. It took me years to even understand the reality. She has always been there for me no matter the circumstances. I often cried when I thought about the past, and then I would call my mom, sobbing on the phone and apologising for not seeing the truth. I believe my mom was desperate for me to see her as a friend when I was a teenager, and it must have been hard for her to watch me chase something she knew was not realistic. I admit I wasn't true and realistic to myself, which may have caused me hurt in the end. At the time, my friend's opinion meant more to me than my mom's opinion. But now the tables have turned, and my mom's opinion is highly appreciated. I believe when we have our own kids and are now the parent, we tend to see exactly what our parents were talking about.

Why didn't we listen? It's because we had to experience life for ourselves, and now we have, we can make the necessary changes. When you see your child chasing a friend like they are the only people in their lives, it can be very hard to deal with. We must remember that we all go through these stages, and we must allow our kids to walk their own journey. How else will they learn? They too must decide which path they are willing to take in friendship. Remember everyone has their own story to tell.

I also realised that I am no longer an only child. My dream was answered nine years ago. I have a brother; whether we are close or not, that cannot change the fact that we are blood-related. I realised that this delusional mindset must stop, and I am the only one that has control over every choice I make.

This is my journey and my story that I choose to share.

## The Realisation:

- I am no longer lonely; I was never lonely.
- You cannot please people all the time.
- If you know that you have been the best person you can be, never let someone make you feel anything less.
- If someone sees you as a friend who is always putting them down, then it's just not meant to be. Do not dedicate your life trying to prove otherwise.
- It's okay to say no.
- Put your friends in the right categories.
- It's okay not to tell a close friend your personal business.
- Put up boundaries and don't let people take advantage of you.
- People make mistakes.
- Friends with different morals may struggle to sustain connection due to numerous disagreements.
- Friends who speak to you without respect are not your friends.
- A jealous friend is dangerous.
- Too many friends can cause confusion and distress.
- Insecurities break friendships.
- Never assume, just ask directly.
- Friendship is a two-way road
- You cannot judge a friend's actions based on what you would do.
- Friends can disappoint you from time to time.
- If you are constantly arguing and falling out, then that's a sign that you are not compatible.
- It's normal to lose friends.

# Chapter 14
# Accepting and Adjusting

I had to accept all the points that I listed in The Realisation chapter. Realising doesn't mean that you are going to accept and adjust straight away. It took me time to detox myself from my toxic mindset. Once I changed my mindset, I was able to accept and adjust. I often wondered if I was the toxic person in my friendships because I was not realistic. This dream of a perfect and long-lasting friendship caused me to overthink everything. I accept that losing my friends might be beneficial for us all. I accept that until I adjusted my mindset, I couldn't sustain a healthy relationship.

There was a time when there was a serious pandemic, and we all had to stay indoors for more than three months without socialising. I was stuck with my family and my thoughts, which caused me to overthink. I did a lot of self-reflecting, which prompted me to look back on my childhood days, and I tried to analyse why I carry certain traits. I sometimes noticed when I thought about my past, I cried, and for some reason, I felt much better, it was very therapeutic. I often wondered if I was crying because I never really cried about it before, so my body subconsciously allowed me to release something that was inside me that I wasn't aware of. I like to do a little bit of psychology on myself to see why I am the person I am today. Some days, I felt like my thoughts were going to drive me crazy. I can confirm that if you do not have a healthy mind, you cannot sustain a healthy relationship.

Have you ever met someone who is always sad, angry, and depressed? The simplest things annoy them, which causes them to act out of character. It is very clear that they have personal issues that they need to work on within their lives, and until they solve these issues, they will always be angry and hurt. Hurt people cause hurt to others without even realising their actions.

It wasn't easy to adjust to being by myself without a close friend because I wasn't used to it, but I believe the pandemic forced me to accept and adjust. I chose to change, and it did not happen instantly, but it was the stepping-stone to something new. I admit some days I felt lonely, and I wished I had a close friend that I could do more with because the majority of my friends were far away. I realised that the obsession of wanting a sisterly bond would slowly try to sneak its way back into my thoughts. I learnt that we do not have to be all alone, we can socialise with people and occasionally plan events to meet up.

The cycle of life allows you to meet and greet new people, you do not have to lock yourself away from the world. My new motto was, have a drink, have a laugh, have fun, and walk away to your separate lives. This assured me that no one gets hurt in this process. I realised I enjoy meeting people and allowing myself to have more of a social life and a new perspective.

Life is complicated as it is and can be stressful, why do I need to have people in my life who bring no value or benefits to the table? I found myself juggling, work, housework, family, friendships, and a relationship. Anyone that was adding more pressure to my life, I would always choose to let them go, regardless of how many years we had been friends. I wanted to simplify my life as much as possible. As I got into my late twenties, I chose healthier relationships.

Losing a friend doesn't make you a bad friend or a bad person. It is normal to lose friends, I always thought if I lost a friend, I was a failure, because I failed to have a long-lasting imaginary sister. Sisters are supposed to remain sisters for life because once you are blood-related, that will never change the fact that you are sisters. This was my theory, so if I didn't manage to keep a sister, then I had failed. Let's be honest there are so many siblings that haven't even exchanged words for years. If this is possible, then losing a friend must be normal.

Losing a friend isn't a bad thing because it causes you to spend more time with yourself. It also allows you to get rid of toxic friends who affect your happiness and peace. Toxic friends can keep you stuck in the same place or cycle. When you lose a friend, it improves your social life for the better. It opens the opportunity for meeting new people and having a different perspective on life, it can also allow you to try new things. Losing a friend forces you to put your efforts into the right people.

Life is short, and we do not have much time on this earth, we never know the hour or day we will be gone, so why not make the most of it. We should always try to enjoy our lives to the fullest, no matter the circumstance.

A quick review of my life, I lost:

- Friends from the buddy crew
- The helpful friend
- The knowledgeable friend
- The popular friend

And I am left with:

- My mom
- My husband and kids
- My cousin
- The companion friend
- The inspirational friend
- The supportive friend
- The positive friend
- The acquaintance

No expectation is our remedy, and we all have something in common: maintaining healthier relationships. We don't have time for disagreements or people who are always offended, we do not have time for people who want to complicate our lives. We are just looking for someone to be genuine and to motivate us to be the best.

Then I have a range of people I associate myself with, we occasionally meet up at each other's events and give support when needed. The best thing about these relationships is that we are not involved in each other's personal lives. Even though my best friend from St. Maarten, and I do not talk very often, she will always be in my heart, and that love for her will never change. She allowed me to understand the full concept of friendship.

I mean, what more do I want? I have lost friends, but that's not a negative factor. They were good people, but sometimes things happen, it might not be what I wanted, but I must learn to accept and adjust. They assisted me in becoming a better person, and they allowed me to be realistic with myself. I thank them for being a part of my journey because they have been there in my times of need and we shared great memories.

When I analyse the people that are left in my life, the majority of them are abroad. I often wonder if it would be different if I was back there with them? **The biggest acceptance** is that even though I am left with a few people, our friendship is still not promised. I will leave time to be the judge. People change, and circumstances change, which allows friendships to change. In every situation, we must accept the reality and adjust to be the best person we can be.

I noticed a pattern in the type of people I was attracted to; they were either an only child or the only girl among siblings.

Sometimes we think having loads of friends is a good thing, but when things get rough, and you look around, how many of them are there to give you a helping hand to support you? When you keep many friends, they may not always be genuine and have an interest in your wellbeing. We must learn to put our friends in their categories. For example, if you have a friend that solely cares about partying and just doesn't take life seriously, do not expect them to be there to listen to your problems or be a helping hand. We get hurt because we are not analysing the types of friends we have. This type of friend is there to lift your spirits up when you are down, they don't necessarily need to know what is going on in your life. Utilise them for what they are good at (partying), instead of getting upset and complicating life.

As I grew older, my true friends also became fewer. Truth be told, solid friendships are rare to find, so I ask which path do you take when it comes to friendship? I choose to walk down the path of peace and happiness but also accepting that there will be ups and downs in any relationship. I have full control of who is part of my journey. I have finally found a strategy for how to let go and accept the reality of life. Try to make good judgements and allow time to take its course because none of our friends are guaranteed for life. In a heartbeat, things can change, so forgive often, and love with all your heart.

*Love is the greatest power on earth - it conquers all things!*

# Finding Your Path in Friendship

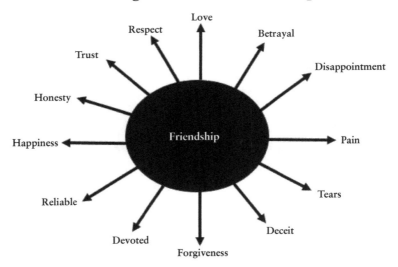

The advantages and disadvantages of friendship

Follow my Instagram page

@author2020

**And**

Subscribe to my website to share your experiences of real-life situations. This platform allows people from all over the world to come together to express themselves.
**You are never alone!**

www.therealityoflife.online

# About the Author

Sarafina James is a wife and mother of two, who balances a full-time job in Health and Safety with her family-run gift basket business. She enjoys cooking and being creative, and makes family her number one priority, believing that showing love to one another is an essential part of life-happiness.

She lives the dream of traveling the world, eating out; even being adventurous from time to time. She has a passion for helping others and decided to turn this passion into a writing form; hoping that it may help others to identify their own true potential and worth. A realist to life, who is trying to build a platform to help people from all over the world, Sarafina continues to discover different techniques to improve herself to become a better person, recognising that in life there is always room for improvement.